# The Butterfly Factor

A fable by:
Carol Grace Anderson, M.A.

Rock Hill Publishing
Nashville, TN

Published by
Rock Hill Publishing
P.O. Box 148258
Nashville, TN 37214-8258

Call toll-free to order:
877-446-9364
or online
**Butterflyfactor.com**

Fax: 615-885-2466
E-mail: RockHillBooks@aol.com

Illustrations: Mary Beth Anderson

Consulting Editor: Barbara Rick
Book design: Gena Kennedy
Editor: Ramona Richards

Printed in the United States of America

ISBN  0-9660276-4-7

This book is dedicated
to my parents,
Rev. Jim and Lois Anderson,
who have encouraged me
and countless others
to see the light…
and fly to new heights.

# Acknowledgements

Thank you Mary Beth for leaving behind such divine artwork. You are soulful indeed. We're grateful to share your inspired creations. We miss you lots. Keep those feathers coming!

To the Anderson, Gage, and Blea families: Your endless love and encouragement compel me. You are phenomenal.

To those who brighten my journey and put wings on my world: I treasure our friendship.

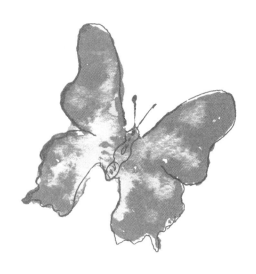

# The Beginning

And the mother butterfly left two eggs in the middle of a damp leaf. She lightly flew away toward the clear, blue sky.

The forest was quiet.

"Anybody out there?" said one egg…its velvety voice breaking the silence.

"Well, I'm not really *out* there," answered the other. "But I'm here, unfortunately. What's going on? Who are you anyway?"

"I'm Bettina. Is it dark where you are, too?"

"Yeah…and cold!"

"It's a good chance to be still," she answered.

"Uh, what's the punch line?" mumbled the unhappy voice.

"Listen," he continued, "just a short time ago, I was warm, safe, and I always felt my momma's heartbeat. Now I'm stuck here. Why ME for Pete's sake?"

"Well, Pete, I guess that's a good question," Bettina replied with a chuckle.

"No, no, my name's Buster".

"Oh, Buster. Cute. Buster what?"

"Butterfly. A family name, I guess."

"You're kidding! I have the same exact last name. In fact, I think Mom named me Bettina because it went so nicely with Butterfly."

"Where in the world are we?" he asked. "This could be the end of the world! The end of me! How do we get out of this terrible mess?"

"Buster, this is different, yes. But who knows? Instead of the end, this could be the beginning. Might as well live it up."

"Betty, this is no time to be making light of serious circumstances."

"It's Bettina, and it's been a long day. I think I'm gonna call it a day—or night—whatever."

# If this is life... live it up!

Buster was flustered. He swam around his place looking in every nook and cranny for a way out. Exhausted, he worked on a plan of escape.

Bettina drifted off to sleep—floating like a feather inside the safety of her shell.

She dreamed of a lovely copper-colored ladybug who was sending her messages about life. Not completely clear...but intriguing.

As she slowly awoke, Bettina saw writing on the outside of her tiny house. The sunlight illuminated the words: "You are an egg. Very important in the whole scheme of things. Right now you're living in a shell. We all start somewhere. Bye for now, LB."

# We all start somewhere!

Bettina thought about that as the sun warmed her small dwelling.

"So, what now?" Buster cried out.

"I don't know. I'm just taking it easy over here."

"Are you losing it like I am? I've about had it with this small space."

"You may not believe it, but something is written on the outside of my house."

"Yeah—that's a good one."

"Really, Buster! It says I'm an egg...and that I'm important in the big picture."

"Well, if you're so important, I'd like to see you get me out of here."

"Unfortunately, I don't think I can. The message was from LB. It said I'm living in a shell."

"Maybe your shell is scrambling you. You're saying that someone named LB is giving you inside information?"

"During my rest, I dreamed that I was getting some sort of communication."

"And just who appeared in your cosmic dream?"

"A ladybug."

"Oh, no wonder the message was signed 'LB.' That's short for ladybug."

"Hey, Detective Buster. Maybe you could help me figure out the rest of it."

"What I want to know is...how did I land here...and where do I get a ticket to go right back where I was? Now *that's* important."

He continued, "If you find out anything, let me know. It's my turn to get some shut-eye."

# Messages come in all kinds of packages

Bettina meditated inside her small, cozy shell. It was becoming darker outside and a few rays from the sunset cast a rich, golden color all around her.

Beautiful shadows formed on the oval walls. The one that caught her eye first was a colorful figure flying through the air.

"So free," she thought.

Bettina's imagination flew alongside that winged creature. Into fresh, green meadows. Over peaceful ponds. Into a beautiful castle filled with more brilliant colors and fragrances than she had ever imagined.

There was a quiet knocking on the outside of her shell. Bettina responded, "Yes, hello out there. Can you hear me through the wall?"

"Loud and clear, Ms. Egg. This is LB. By the way, I'm a good bug. And I know you'd be considered what we call a good egg."

"Thanks! Is LB short for Ladybug? Buster figured it out. My neighbor's smart but miserable."

"Ah, some folks choose to be upset with every circumstance that comes their way. We don't always choose the circumstance, but we always choose the response."

"Bettina Butterfly is my full name—passed down from my grandmother. I have lots of her traits."

"And yet we're all wonderfully unique. Look deeper and you'll see a treasure."

# We don't always choose the circumstances. But we always choose the response.

"I'll be thinking about that during my afternoon float in here.

Where do you live, Ladybug?"

"I have several residences, but my main place is a lush, green leaf nearby. I'm on my way to pick up a few aphids for lunch on my way home."

"Thanks for stopping by...and remember, you're always welcome."

"I appreciate that, Bettina."

In the quietness, Bettina was soaking in all she had just heard. So simple yet powerful.

# Look deeper... and you'll see a treasure.

"Hey—it's me," Buster grumbled.

"Oh? What's going on over there?"

"Nothing, of course! Same old thing every day. A bug tried to visit me, too. That's how off-the-wall things are getting!"

"What did you do about the bug thing?"

"I told it to knock it off, don't bug me, and don't even think of coming back."

Bettina drifted into dreamy sleep.

In early morning she awoke to birds chirping nearby. Wake-up songs with beautiful melodies. One would sing a line, and another would answer in harmony.

The music inspired Bettina to create lyrics:

> **Another lovely day**
> **to sing and to fly.**
> **Someday we will all**
> **meet in the sky...**

"What, are you having some kind of party over there?" Buster yelled.

"You might call it a 'music party'," she said with a giggle.

"No such thing in my book."

"Buster, you could rewrite your book any way you want to."

"Nah…I'd rather sleep all day so I can forget this horrible place I'm in."

# You can always rewrite your own book.

"What DO you like, Buster?"

"Sleep…so I can zone out. And right now I can't even do that!"

Bettina listened again for the singing of the birds. They were silent now. Buster's loud voice had hushed them.

Bettina floated in the midday light. Now she could make out a brilliant mosaic design on the upper part of her shell.

Transfixed by this world, she imagined that she frolicked with colorful creatures, rode huge elephants, and ate mounds of magical forest delights.

Wistfully, Bettina drifted off to blissful sleep.

"Anybody home?" whispered Ladybug the next morning.

"Yes…I'm so happy to hear your voice. How are you doing, LB?"

"Better now! That egg next door to you is a real stick-in-the-mud. He keeps telling me to 'bug out'. I can take a hint."

"So, he's an egg, too?"

"Sure is."

"Buster would like his old life back. Come to think of it, I don't think he was very thrilled about those times either."

Ladybug smiled and shook her head.

"You know, Bettina…there's always a nice sur-
prise just right around the corner."

"There aren't any corners here in my shell, but I
have my share of nice surprises."

"You're open to them. You notice them. And I
notice I must be on my way. Enjoy!"

# Nice surprises
# are right
# around
# the corner.

"Hey, Buster. Are you awake?"

"I'll say! I didn't get one moment of sleep."

"Birds too loud again?"

"Oh, no. To tell you the truth, I've been very worried."

"Worried about what, Buster?"

"I'm scared I'll be in this boring place forever."

"My friend, Ladybug, says you're an egg, like me. Can you try to make your life more enjoyable? Meet some new folks? Try some new things?"

"Why? There's absolutely nothing to enjoy. It's not even worth trying."

"Excuse me, BBBBuster, but I gotta go. Talk to you later."

Bettina was breathless. From a sudden surge of incredible strength, her whole body was pushing against all the walls of the tiny space.

In the next instant, Bettina felt her head move right through the top of her shell. There was no time for fear...and besides...it felt right.

Bettina opened her eyes. The view was so awesome it was startling.

Flowers danced in the sun.

Meadows burst with exquisite colors...more beautiful than her dream.

Graceful branches framed rolling brooks...creating enchanting sounds.

Wild strawberries created a scarlet carpet.

# Sometimes... the simplest things in life are the most powerful.

The air was so fresh and sweet.

Bettina could see that she had a furry coat, a scaly tummy, and tiny legs. When she even thought about moving, her whole body automatically moved.

"This is simply amazing!" she cried out.

Looking around, she saw no sign of her last home. She did see an oval object on a leaf nearby and heard sounds coming from there.

Bettina wiggled over. "Hello?" she said.

"Bettina, is that you? You sound different...like you're closer."

"Buster, now I can actually see where you live!"

"Are you hallucinating again?"

"No. No. The wildest thing happened. Now the world is huge. It's all different and hard to describe. It's the best!"

# Enjoy!

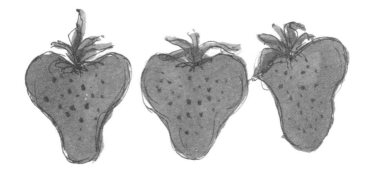

# The Journey

"You're not making any sense, Bettina. I think you could use some fresh air."

"There's a *world* full of fresh air out here. Can you imagine it?"

"I can imagine how much better my life would be if I didn't have to live here."

"I don't mean to spoil this party, Buster, but I've got things to see, places to go, friends to meet, new food to eat…and I don't even know what else!"

"Sounds overwhelming to me."

"I'll drop by later if that's all right."

"Oh, I guess so," Buster muttered.

When Bettina returned just before sunset, she noticed something new.

"Hello, furry guy."

"Bettina! It's me...Buster!"

"Buster, I would never have known you except for that low voice of yours. When did you arrive out here?"

"Just now. The pull was too strong for me to fight it. Just as I started to panic and yell for help, my head broke through a crack in the side of my shell. Terrible!

"In shock, I finally opened up my eyes to this scary place," he continued.

Buster was confused by all the new sounds and scents coming from every direction. And now he began to notice all the fresh air that Bettina had described.

"I don't like it one bit. I do know that this furry thing around me is ridiculous. And these crazy things on my belly have got to go."

"Oh, that furry thing is a good place to live…and the little legs can really take you places."

"There you go, Bettina. Imagining things again."

"I've decided to celebrate being here. I'm off."

# Celebrate being here!

Bettina wiggled away on a new adventure. Down a pathway in the forest, she came upon a fern growing near the base of a tree. Nestled under the greenery was a group of furry creatures resembling Bettina.

"Good afternoon, Cat!" they yelled in unison. "Are you one of the new neighbors we've heard about?"

"I'm not sure. I recently arrived here. My name is Bettina. What a great place this is! Did you think I was someone else?"

"We call all the new caterpillars 'Cat' for short...but not for long. Just a little joke. Our small fern group likes to laugh. Everyone has a specialty."

"That's good news. And you say I'm a caterpillar now? I used to be an egg."

"Eggs-actly."

"Ha. You're fun! By the way, since I'm new here, do you have any advice for me?"

"Yes, indeed. Two things to avoid at all costs: rubber tires and shoe soles. They take their toll. We've heard of population control, but they're over the top."

"How do you survive them?"

"Be mindful of your surroundings. Watch where you're going. And avoid the mean creatures...they want you for supper."

"Anything else?"

# Watch where you're going.

"Don't ever stop having fun!" said one of the caterpillars.

"Life is short. Live large," said another.

"Just BE here. This moment is an instant you'll never have again. The more you live with that in mind, the greater your life will be."

"I'll be moving on—and of course, living large."

"The only way to go! And please take this snack with you as a gift."

Bettina slowly inched her way down the path trying to absorb all the sights at once. She came across a small flat rock that had been warmed by the sun. The perfect spot to rest for a minute.

Bettina unfolded her gift. It was a small leaf with many tiny insects inside. Curious, she took a small bite. Not sure if she liked the flavor, she took another bite. *Hmmm, not too bad,* she thought as she finished it—leaf and all.

As night set in, Bettina Butterfly crawled into a small, safe space under an exposed tree root, and slept soundly.

# Live
# large.

"Buzzzzzz, buzzzzz," was a new sound that greeted Bettina the next morning. She opened her eyes to see a strange-looking creature covered with some yellow and black fuzz...and wings, too. It was visiting each little wild flower in a patch near Bettina's sleeping spot.

"Hi there, Buzzy," she offered.

Surprised, the bumblebee slowed down and looked over toward the voice. "How did you know my name was Busy?"

"Oh, I didn't call you Busy...I called you Buzzy because of the unusual noise you were making. It was just a guess."

"You know—I kind of like that name better than what I was stuck with. But I'll lose the 'y' and just go with Buzz. That sounds cool. And who might you be?"

"My name's Bettina. I'm fairly new around here. Already, I can see that there's so much going on!"

"I'll say. The action never stops."

"So, why were you first named Busy?"

"Some folks refer to us as 'busy bees' because we spend a lot of time pollinating flowers."

"Poli...what?"

"It means we help flowers grow. They're all so different and beautiful. Some even have heavenly fragrances. Not a bad job, huh?"

"For sure. Sounds like you're doing important work...helping the world smell lovely."

"Bettina, we're all vital when we think about our part of the big puzzle."

"And you mean the puzzle of life. It all seems to fit together in the long run, doesn't it?"

"Precisely," Buzz answered. "Now, as pleasant as this is...I must get busy and fly on to my next bouquet."

"You mean, you actually fly?"

"Yes indeed, Bettina. You see, I'm not *supposed* to fly. Many folks believe that my body shape and short wingspan would make it impossible. But someone forgot to tell me and all the other bees. We tried the impossible. And guess what? We fly!"

"That's great Buzz. Fly high."

# Try
# the
# impossible.

Bettina gave her fur a good shake for the day and wiggled off...back toward Buster.

A lazy brook flowed alongside the path, and Bettina stopped to rest. She was surrounded by soft petals with huge drops of stray brook water. They looked like crystal bubbles.

Bettina tried a drop. Then drank another. *Delicious...and there will always be plenty*, she thought to herself.

Back on the path, she kept an eye and ear out for Buster. She saw no sign of him and was almost back at the starting point.

Bettina put a little more zip in her wiggle, hoping to reach him before nightfall.

As she approached the familiar spot, she saw a small, curled-up ball of fur.

As Bettina edged over to study it in more detail, a low voice asked, "Bet, is that you?"

"Yes, yes, it's me, Buster. Nice to see you again."

"Well, where did you go running off to? You know, you could get hurt—even killed in a frightening place like this!"

"You just stayed here, Buster?"

"I have no place to go. This is worse than the last place. That shell was small, but you could at least grab some peace and quiet now and then."

"Oh, Buster, if you just took a short journey right around here...you'd see a world that is indescribable!"

# Look around. You'll see a world that is indescribable!

"Sounds like you're having those weird dreams again. I've got to have something to eat…and that's no dream."

"You're one lucky Buster. I met some other caterpillars and they showed me where to find food—the good stuff."

"Caterpillars? Is that some club you've joined out here?"

"No, that's what we are now. We were eggs, now we're caterpillars. We look different than before…but they told me, we're still us. Same *beings*. Different *outfits*."

"Enough hocus pocus. Where's the grub?"

"Here's the big secret Buster…there's good food all around us."

"Yeah? I'm so sure of that!"

"No kidding. Let's shimmy over to that patch of buttercups and leaves for some dinner. We'll be aristocratic…dining so late in the evening."

"I'm hungry enough to eat a tree. Forget the sophistication, Bettina."

"You know, it's funny, Buster. We are eating, well…part of the tree, anyway. These leaves are luscious. And see these tiny squirming things on some of them? They really top off a great meal."

"C'mon…this food is nothing to write home about, but it'll keep us alive for another humdrum day."

With full tummies, the two caterpillars moved toward some soft grass and fell asleep.

The lovely sounds of the forest woke Bettina at dawn. "I'll be back later, Buster. Make it a beautiful day."

She inched her way toward a new pathway. The birds were singing like a choir. Bettina remembered the harmonious melody they sang when she was an egg.

# Make
# it a
# beautiful
# day!

As she moved along the path framed with big, magnificent rocks, she heard a familiar voice.

"Bettina, is that really you?" asked the loving LB.

"Ladybug! I'm so glad to see you again."

"Likewise. I'm getting older now and I don't have quite the energy I used to have. How have you been doing?"

"There's so much going on here! I'm trying to take it all in."

"Way to go, Bettina. Uh oh! I hear it coming."

"What is that loud noise, Ladybug?"

"That, my friend, is a lawnmower. It's coming our way. Those blades can tear us to shreds."

"What do we do?"

"Move out of the way...fast! Could you give me a lift?"

Ladybug crawled onto Bettina's back. As they moved toward safety, LB pointed out a beautiful, white feather alongside the path.

"A feather is a precious thing, Bettina. It represents freedom and flight. Sometimes one will just appear...like a kiss from heaven."

They made it to the safety of a rock ledge.

"If it weren't for *you*, I may have been a goner! By working together we can get wonderful results. There's power in numbers."

"Yes, I see, LB. You're wise."

"But smarts wouldn't have helped, if you hadn't wiggled us to safety. Now I must take my afternoon snooze. Have a nice trip down the trail."

# A feather is like a kiss from heaven.

Bettina took a few sips of cool puddle water. How delicious it tasted after such fast wiggling.

She noticed a strange-looking, flying creature nearby.

"New in these parts, huh?" the stranger asked Bettina.

"How did you know?"

"I can see lots of stuff from up here. I would have remembered a beautiful caterpillar like you."

"Why, thank you. Who—or what—are you?"

"I'm a dragonfly. They call me 'Dreamboat'."

"You are an attractive durrrr."

"Dragonfly."

"I see that you fly, but where did the dragon come from?"

"Never could figure that out. Maybe that's why they started that 'Dreamboat' thing."

"Since I've been here, I've noticed that there's something special about everyone. What's your area of expertise?"

"Watch this!"

# There's something special about everyone!

Bettina was amazed at the flying tricks the dragonfly could do. Diving up, down, and all around.

"What do you do when you reach your destination?"

"I eat dangerous insects. The fewer the bad bugs in your path, the better it is for you. But to me, they're just plain good eatin'."

"Thanks for helping the planet, Dreamboat. I must be going, but maybe we'll meet again."

"There's no maybe about it, gorgeous."

# Stay away from the bad bugs.

Bettina headed for a patch of bright dandelions. As she went over a few sharp pebbles, her furry coat fell away.

A brand new fur exterior, even more rich and beautiful than the last, replaced it. *How did this happen?* she wondered.

Bettina took a rest among the sea of dandelions…trying to make sense of her new coat.

"Good day," came a high-pitched voice.

"Hope I didn't wake you, Ma'am."

"Oh, I was resting here...trying to figure it all out. I'm Bettina Butterfly."

"I live in a colony with many other ants...but I'm the only 'Antoine'. There's always so much to do, I rarely take a break. But we ALL need to slow down now and then. Balance is best. What were you contemplating?"

"See, I had a nice fur coat, then it just fell off and there was this spectacular fur under it."

"You're evolving before your very eyes, Bettina."

"Come again?  What's evolving?"

"Going through life stages. We all do it. Look at these dandelions. Aren't they a brilliant yellow?

Now look over there...see those cute puffy round things on a stem? They're the same flowers in a different stage of life. The wind blows the seeds from those fluffy things and new dandelions form."

"That kind of makes sense because I was an egg at one time."

"I was born to work hard along with my neighbors for the good of the colony—and to make room for newborn ants. Working together works wonders."

"So, you must have lots of ants and uncles?" she joked.

"Yep. You're a lot of fun, Bettina. It's been nice to have a break in the action, but I better get back on the job."

"Give my best to your colony, Antoine."

# Working together works wonders.

Energized by the visit, Bettina began making her way back toward home. She felt sad that Buster wouldn't be interested. If he only knew what he was missing!

Rain started falling, making the path muddy and slow. The cool drops felt soft and soothing on her new, fur wrap.

As she approached the spot where she left Buster, she could see a curled-up ball of fur. It was unfamiliar.

"Hello?" she asked quietly.

"Oh, Bettina, you're back. If I hadn't heard your voice, I wouldn't have recognized you. I've told you before that you shouldn't go off like that. Who knows what you might find?"

"Precisely! Hey, Buster, you have a beautiful new coat, too!"

"Eh, I didn't much care for the other one and now they lay this one on me. It's ridiculous."

"No, it's evolution."

"Schmevolution! There's nothing at all new around here except this hideous, new fur...and scary-looking creatures everywhere."

"Yes, aren't they interesting? I brought us some food. The rain makes everything taste even better."

"Wetter, not better!"

# We choose our views.

After a refreshing night's rest under some sheltering branches, Bettina awoke at dawn to explore some more.

The rising sun was beginning to peek out from the clouds. Everything looked so bright and alive.

"Top of the morning to you," came a rich voice from some tall grass.

Bettina stopped and looked around but saw absolutely nothing.

As she started to move on, a funny-looking green thing hopped onto the path.

"Do you have to leave already? You just got here," said the unfamiliar voice.

"You move in such an bouncy way. Where did you learn that?" asked Bettina.

"It's called hopping. It works for me. Actually, it's not the only way I get around. I fly, too. I'm what they call a praying mantis."

"How did you get a handle like that?"

"Watch. When I'm still, it looks like I'm praying. By the way, my name is Mellow. And you would be?"

"Bettina. I'm a caterpillar."

"Cat-a-what?"

"Caterpillar."

"Oh, yes, yes, I've heard good things about you folks."

"I'm fairly new around here. You said something about praying? What is that?"

"Talking to God. See, there's a power way bigger than you and me. The answer to a lot of important questions. He created you even before you were an egg."

 _____

# There's a
# bigger
# power.

_____

"I sensed there was something divine going on all along, Mellow."

"You can always trust your gut instincts. When you don't honor them…that's when you can get into some tricky, sticky, situations."

"What is it like to have wings?"

"Don't know what I'd do without 'em, Bettina. I don't use them that much, but they're there when I need them!"

"When is that?"

"When the bad bugs are out of my reach. I'm one of the good guys. I take care of those pests that might get in your way."

"Thank you, Mellow. You sure have given me lots to ponder as I wiggle on my way."

Bettina's heart and mind were full as she continued her journey. She felt incredibly abundant.

It was close to lunchtime by the time Bettina paused to catch her breath and look for a bite to eat.

As she began nibbling on the second delicious blade of grass, she heard some familiar voices.

54

# Trust your gut instinct.

"Is that you, Cat? I see you have a different coat. Nice!" one of them said. "And I see it's starting to show some wear. You must be getting around a lot...that's good."

Bettina looked toward the voice in a nearby flower patch. There they were...some of the old caterpillar buddies laughing and having a wonderful time.

"Welcome back," they said in unison.

"Oh, you remember me."

"Sure, Baroka. I've got an incredible memory," one of them said.

"Uh, it's Bettina."

"I never remember a name, but I always forget a face," another chuckled.

"And I'm new to the caterpillar group," came a silky, unfamiliar voice. "They call me Lorie Lounger."

Another said, "Bettina, fill us in on what you've been up to."

"Well, it's great to see you again! I don't think I met all of you before."

"Right…some have just joined us. Some have new furs. Some have gone to the great beyond."

"Where is that?"

"Maybe it's the great forest in the sky. At some point, one of the bunch will just up and disappear. Without even a lousy goodbye!"

"Hmm. Could it be that they don't really mind going?"

"Maybe they've had it up to here with corny jokes. So, tell us what's new, Bettina?"

"Every day is different and interesting. It's just *fabulous* here."

"So, why don't you like it?" asked another with a wink.

# Teachers show up at just the right time.

"Ha! That's cute."

"I hope you've met some of our fascinating neighbors."

"Yes, indeed—one right after another. Teachers seem to show up at just the right time."

"You got it. Now, our little group here has ALL the answers...but nobody ever asks us any questions!" one said smiling. "Who have you run into?"

The group was enraptured as Bettina shared the details of her adventures.

They invited her to stay, but as the sun began to set, she reluctantly went on her way.

"I must move on. I'll never forget what you told me a long time ago...live large!"

At the edge of the pathway, Lorie stopped Bettina and whispered: "They live large. I *lounge* large, darlin'."

Darkness set in. Bettina was weary and her legs were tired. She curled up on a soft leaf and fell fast asleep.

A relentless, buzzing sound awoke her at dawn. She looked up thinking it might be her old friend Buzz the bumblebee.

Instead, angry flying creatures began swarming all around her making irritating sounds she never heard before. One began stinging her.

"Help! I need help!" she shouted out to the forest as another began stinging.

"Dreamboat to the rescue. These mosquitoes are a job for a dragonfly."

Dreamboat hovered over Bettina until the last pesky bug flew away.

"Whew, am I glad to see you!"

"Hey, everyone needs help sometimes. You just have to ask."

"Why were they after me? Were they afraid?"

"Maybe we should call you 'Bettina the dangerous'!"

"Yeah...I'm dangerous all right!"

"Mosquitoes thrive on the sweetness of others. They're bloodsuckers."

"They must think I'm sweet."

"No doubt. Along with your beauty, I like your spunk, Bettina. You're out there…really living. Those who don't take chances in life, miss so much!"

"Yes, I guess you're right. I never thought of it that way."

"You're safe now. I don't want to get in the way of your adventures. I certainly hope we'll meet again down the road. Meanwhile, happy travels."

"I can't thank you enough, Dreamboat," she said.

The dragonfly flew away—showing off some of his fancy, flying techniques.

# Everyone needs help sometimes. Just ask.

Real
living
includes
taking
chances.

# The Transition

Bettina inched forward, cautiously. She stopped at a patch of violets. Soft petals and brilliant purple hues. She tasted one. "Mmm, delicious," she said out loud. "I'll have to come back when I'm hungry."

Still a little shaky from her mosquito skirmish, Bettina curled up in the shelter of a nearby rock.

A deafening clap of thunder interrupted the stillness. Bright, strange bolts of light danced around the forest. Wind began blowing so hard, it whistled and roared through the trees. And rain came down like a wall of water.

Bettina shook. Squeezed under a protective rock as far as she could, she stretched her short legs and gripped the ground with all her might.

Trees and branches surrendered to the wind—
banging and falling all around. The roaring rain and
thunder kept on, illuminated by lightning strikes.

She was sure she'd be swept away.

By the time the storm quieted, all her energy was
spent. Bettina closed her eyes and breathed deeply.
She could feel sore places where the edge of the rock
cut through her soaked, thinning fur.

Still weak from her crisis, Bettina felt proud and
strong that she had survived.

"Ah, you made it, of course!" came an old but
warm, familiar voice.

"Oh, Ladybug. I can't tell you how happy I am to
see you!"

"I always knew you were a survivor, Bettina.
Storms show you what you're made of."

"But do they have to be so severe, LB?"

"Sometimes, yes. See all these trees and branch-
es scattered everywhere?"

"What a big mess," Bettina agreed.

"But look over at those gorgeous violets in the patch.

"They may look delicate, but the secret is that during the rough times, they bend. Those big trees would have survived the high winds if they could have flowed with it."

# Storms show you what you're made of.

"Sometimes it's better to bend, Ladybug?"

"You got it. Just look at those big, broken branches and twisted twigs. Then look at those amazing little violets."

"How did you get so smart, LB?"

"We don't learn anything when things are running smoothly. But that is enjoyable, no question about that.

"And, Bettina, speaking of living...I feel that my days here are numbered. When it's time, I'll be ready to go on."

"How can you talk like that, Ladybug?" she asked as her eyes filled with tears.

"Leaving is a very important part of living. Death is not the end. It's the beginning of a new season. Soon you'll become a chrysalis. We'll both change form. No matter what, I'll always know how precious and special you are."

With a heavy heart, Bettina wiggled toward a sweet honeysuckle vine. There, within the beautiful fragrance, she allowed herself the gift of tears.

When she was ready to move on, she thought of Buster. She was concerned about how he had survived the storm. The lovely caterpillar moved as fast as she could to find him.

# Tears are
# a gift
# from the soul.

"Bettina, is that really you?" came a shrill voice.

"Didn't you recognize me, Antoine? How did you survive the storm?"

"Our colony got scattered around, and unfortunately, we lost a few. But we're re-building to come back better than ever. Glad you made it too!"

"Yes, honestly, it was quite a struggle. But now I know how strong I am."

A deep voice interrupted them... "Bettina, you're okay. Whew! I heard your cry for help a while back, but by the time I got there, I didn't see you."

"Hello, Mellow Mantis! Thanks for trying. It was a mess of mosquitoes...hungry ones. A dragonfly came to the rescue."

"And how did you get through the storm?" he asked.

"I found a shelter and held on for dear life. And you?"

"I snuggled into the base of some daffodils. I knew they'd be just fine."

"Right. They're resilient. They can bend and bounce back."

"You've learned a lot, Bettina.

"And Antoine, I see you're back to work already. Can't you chill out for a while?" Mellow asked.

"Not right now. We've got some new, exciting things going on. I need to help lead the crew."

The praying mantis nodded and waved to them both. "Keep on the victory side!" he yelled back as he hopped along his way.

# Keep on the victory side!

Bettina moved forward, hoping to find Buster. She wanted to make it before dark. Crickets were already beginning to make their noise.

Just as she headed around a curve, she saw an impressive caterpillar resting by the opening of a narrow tunnel. Its fur was perfection—like her new one was at first. She got closer and was startled when it yelled out something.

"Buster?" she asked hesitantly, hearing a familiar voice.

"Yes. Bettina??? You don't even look the same. What on earth has happened? And where in the world have you been this time? I thought I would die out here alone in this crazy forest."

"That would be a shame. To die before you really lived!"

# That would be a shame. To die before you really lived.

"There's that silly stuff of yours again. So, why did you take off this time?"

"You'd be surprised at everything that's out there! Beauty, lots of wonderful folks, and yes...there's some danger. Now, it's almost dark. Would you like to share a leaf for supper, Buster?"

"Is that the only grub of choice?"

"We could find some lilacs."

"No, that sounds worse!"

Bettina wiggled over to a soft grassy spot and motioned for Buster. As they slowly munched, she asked him how he made it through the treacherous storm.

"I think you left part of your mind back on the trail. There was no storm. I burrowed a narrow tunnel deep into the earth when you left," Buster continued. "Finally, a good place to hide out and sleep in peace and quiet."

Bettina shared some of the details of her colorful adventures —including the storm. He listened nervously.

"But just look at you, Bettina. You look worn out," Buster said when she finished.

"Looking back on it, it's all been worth it. Fantastic really. I'd do it all again. What have you been doing all this time?"

"Nothing—and then more of nothing! It's gotten more dull and lonely by the day."

The next morning at dawn, Bettina encouraged Buster to join her for a trip to a nearby flower patch she had heard about. He reluctantly agreed.

As they passed the base of an old maple tree, Buster abruptly stopped.

"I can't go any farther, Bet. With all you've been through, you must be afraid and tired, too."

"Fear is dreadful, Buster. We've just started, will you *try* to go a little bit farther? You'll get stronger as you go."

# Fear
# is
# dreadful!

"I'll see you when you get back. You're all I have. Be very careful, I'm sure it can be horrendous out there."

Bettina energetically wiggled her way down a cool, fragrant path. (These trips had become easy for her.) She suddenly came upon a whole field of Morning Glories...blue, ivory, pink, lavender. A sea of brilliance.

She inched over to snack on some clover that framed a purple blossom.

"Aha! You found this slice of Paradise," came a buzzing voice from the past. "Aren't we fortunate?"

There was her old buddy, the bumblebee. "You read my mind. How have you been, Buzz?" she asked enthusiastically.

"If I was any better, there'd have to be two of me to handle it. And, of course, in this lovely field, I'm a very busy bee! You've got to get around to get ahead. I see you've been doing that nicely. I'm proud of you."

"Thank you, Buzz. Yes, life is delightful. And we all appreciate your help with these flowers."

# You've got to get around to get ahead.

As she took one last look around, she suddenly got a strong urge to hurry back toward the tree where she left Buster.

When she arrived, she rushed right past him. He was still sleeping. She crawled up the tree to a strong, secure branch and stopped to catch her breath.

At that moment, Bettina noticed a few long strands of rich silk on the branch. Looking closer, she could see many strands. And they were coming straight from her worn fur.

She was amazed as she began to wrap the silk all around her. It felt natural.

Bettina twirled around and around and around until she was completely surrounded by a new home of strong, lovely silk. Her old fur was now gone.

Still stunned by it all, Bettina rested in the quiet darkness of her new dwelling. It reminded her of the season of the egg. These walls also felt sturdy and safe.

After a much-needed rest, she awoke to pleasant music coming from nearby. In the dark, she listened closely. The melody sounded like a familiar song. Bettina began to hum the lyrics that had come to her so long ago:

> **Another lovely day**
> **to sing and to fly.**
> **Someday we will all**
> **meet in the sky...**

Yes, it was a cheerful, morning wake-up song offered by the neighboring birds.

Bettina was thrilled that even in new places, there are some good, familiar traces of the old.

It was the perfect time to recall exquisite details of her journey. She realized that rich adventures require risk. And she felt disheartened, thinking that Buster was probably still sleeping.

The caterpillar could hear soft raindrops fall on the outside shell of her new home. She felt warm and cozy. The steady sound was mesmerizing.

Bettina was relieved to be in a restful place and enjoyed a dreamlike meditation. As she became more wakeful, she heard something from outside.

"Hello?" a young voice whispered. "I'm LB Junior. Ladybug sent me. I'm looking for Bettina Butterfly."

"Uh, yes. I'm Bettina. I'm living in a new type of shell, but it's the same old beautiful me. Just kidding with you. Nice to meet you. I can hear you fine right through the wall."

"Yes, I see you're a chrysalis. That's a nice cocoon you've created."

"Cocoon?"

"Your house.

"Ma'am", he continued, "I'm very sad to say that my Mom left us early this morning. She gave me some parting words and a message she asked me to share with you."

"Ladybug was very special. I'm sorry to see her go...such a dear, wise friend," Bettina said mournfully.

"I buried her in the heart of the most brilliant blue Morning Glory blossom. That's what she wanted."

"How beautiful," Bettina said, with bittersweet tears.

"The message is simply: 'Sometimes the strongest, most loving thing we can do for someone is to do nothing. Just let them go.'"

LB Junior thanked Bettina for her time and left.

*Was Ladybug trying to tell me that I should let her go?* she wondered.

"Help! Bettina, where have you gone? I can't stand this!"

Bettina heard the distant voice of Buster getting closer.

"I'm over here, Buster," she said sniffling.

"No. I don't see you at all. Where exactly are you, for heaven's sake?" he asked frantically as he got closer.

"I'm right in front of you in a new house made of silk. It's a new season…"

Buster cut her off. "But I can't make it without you…your old self… here."

"No matter how I might try to help you, there are some things in life we must learn on our own. I hope you'll want to. It's your choice. You're worth it! Goodbye, Buster," she said wistfully.

Buster Butterfly slowly, quietly inched his way back down to the ground.

# There are some things in life we must learn on our own.

Down below, a friendly voice called out to Buster. "You seem a bit troubled."

"At the end of my rope," Bettina overheard Buster reply, as he choked back tears. "I give up!"

"How can you give up if you never got going?" asked the stranger.

"How would you know?" Buster asked.

"I can see by your confusion—and your perfect, mature coat of fur—you haven't really lived."

"What does living have to do with it? Who are you, anyway?"

Bettina strained to hear more…

"We learn by living through our experiences. Some call me Guy Green, the Generous Grasshopper. It's a mouthful. Who are you?"

"Buster Butterfly. It's a goofy name, I know."

"Quite the contrary. Sounds very fitting."

"What's with that name of yours?" Buster asked hesitantly.

"I don't have a lot of possessions, but I enjoy giving of my time."

"Why?" he asked incredulously.

"When you stop to think about it, it's the most valuable thing we have. Without time, what else is there? How we spend it, is most important."

"But, there's so much danger all around, I've spent most of my time sleeping. That's safer."

"Yes, but it's not living. Maybe that's why you're feeling so down. Come to life!"

# Come to life!

"That's easy to say, but how? I'm feeling so bad, had, mad, and sad, I'll try anything!" Buster replied in desperation.

"Action! That's the very best way to overcome any fear in life. Take action."

"There must be more to it than that. And how would I do that, anyway?" he asked urgently.

"It's quite simple, Buster. See that winding path over there?"

"Uh, yeah," he answered cautiously.

"I suggest you take it. See where it leads. Have fun. I must go now and visit an ailing friend. I'll see you down the road."

The grasshopper started to hop away.

He looked over and saw Buster gradually look around and shake his head. Then the distraught caterpillar took a deep breath and began to slowly wiggle his way down the mysterious path.

In the silence, Bettina wondered if Buster would ever find his way.

# Overcome fear with action!

# The Circle

Some commotion outside caught Bettina's curiosity. Through her cocoon walls, she could hear several high-pitched voices giving orders to each other. It sounded like they were working hard.

"Thanks for the help! I couldn't have done it without you folks," came a smooth, muffled voice. Then all was silent.

Bettina relaxed in the quiet darkness and tried to make sense of it. So much had been happening. She wondered how her fur coat had turned to silk...then a sturdy house.

Now, she could feel her body slowly becoming soft...almost liquid.

The former caterpillar wondered if LB Junior looked just like his Mom. Was he that rich copper color? She wished they could have visited longer.

Bettina could hear and sense that right outside her cocoon, life was going on. Full of interesting stuff. Full of change. Lessons from the past, living in the present.

# Things constantly change.

"Anyone within ear shot?" came a soft, muted voice Bettina had heard.

"Well, I'm over here in a cocoon. I can hear you."

"Oh, I'm right next door," said the smooth voice. "I passed you on my way here...with my work crew."

"What do you mean?" asked Bettina.

"Well, my gorgeous fur was turning into long strands of crazy stuff. I was getting all stuck in it, so I asked some ants passing by to give me a hand.

"Actually, they did it all willingly. They were more than happy to work until my house was completed."

"Sounds like you were once a caterpillar, too."

"Yes, my friends call me Lorie Lounger. They say I'm lazy, which is a huge exaggeration. I just love watching others do the work. What's your name?"

"Bettina Butterfly. We met quite some time ago—you had just joined the caterpillar group. I dropped by for a visit."

"Oh, of course. I remember you. You are quite an adventurer. I guess we both sound different in these houses."

"I'm grateful for the restful time here. It's a nice change," said Bettina.

"For me it's business as usual. I lounge around day and night…the good life. I'm going back to sleep. See you later," she said dreamily.

Bettina felt that between naps, she should start moving this soft new body of hers. She gently pressed against the walls and flexed tiny arm-like things that were forming. She felt spirited yet peaceful.

During her deep sleep that night, Bettina dreamed she visited with Ladybug. Heavenly to see her again!

"How—and where—are you?" she asked LB excitedly.

"I'm better than ever. Light as a feather. And not really far away."

"That could be a song, Ladybug. By the way, I met your son. What a nice guy. And thanks for your message. It already came in handy."

"I'm glad to see you enjoying this season. Stay strong, you'll need it. I'll see you down the line."

"Wait, Ladybug. How will I be sure that you'll visit again?"

"Believe!"

With that, LB vanished and Bettina awoke.

# Believe!

Again, the chrysalis began to press her new, little arms and legs against the wall...over and over again. She could feel her whole body gaining strength.

"I guess you're awake. I can hear you moving around," Lorie called out.

"Yes, I'm giving my new body a workout. I don't want to be a softy. How 'bout you?"

"Notice how workout starts with work. Not for me," she purred.

"Oh, that's right...you're a power lounger! Let's visit later. I gotta go."

As Bettina went back to exercising, she got a burst of super strength. Suddenly the wall she had been pressing against broke wide open.

Stunned and breathless, she looked around at the forest she had left behind.

Now in daylight, Bettina looked down at her new body. Her legs looked small compared with two massive arm-like extensions. They were paper thin and the most glorious colors she had ever seen. Crimson, purple, emerald, gold. Beauty beyond description.

Bettina felt her wings stretch and begin to move. Soon she realized she could make them move. Slower…faster.

She hopped out of her cocoon and onto the branch. Unsteadily, she looked down. *That's a long way!* she thought to herself.

Bettina remembered that some of her old friends had wings. They used theirs to fly.

*Do you suppose I can?* Bettina wondered.

She flapped her wings some more and leaped off the branch in faith.

"Yes, I must believe!" she declared triumphantly, as she flew in a small circle near the home she had just left.

Bettina was anxious to see where these wings would take her.

She took off toward the old familiar pathway and stopped on a dahlia bloom to catch her breath.

*This is a great season!* she smiled to herself.

# It's a great season!

"Hey, beautiful, you must be new in these parts," came a familiar voice.

"Dreamboat, it's me. Bettina."

"Why, Bettina Butterfly. You've changed, but you're as lovely as ever. When did you get your colorful wings?"

"Just today. This is so much fun. I must keep moving."

"Maybe sometime we can fly together," Dreamboat yelled to the butterfly as she flew off.

Bettina's heart began to race when she stopped for a few drops of water and heard a frightening sound. Overhead she saw a cluster of mosquitoes. But, this time her own wings flew her right out their stinging path.

She didn't stop until she got to the sweet honey-suckle vine. She thought she saw Antoine go by but, as usual, he was moving too fast to be sure.

There was a familiar creature resting on a rock nearby.

"Mellow? Are you still praying?" the butterfly asked with a smile.

"What—Bettina? You sure have changed. How are you liking those vibrant wings?"

"One word...sensational! What have you been up to?"

"Trying to do my part to make it a better place—watching for the bad bugs."

"And the world thanks you, Mr. Mellow Mantis. By the way, please say a prayer for my old buddy Buster. I had to let him go. Good seeing you again."

Back at the tree branch where Bettina had built her cocoon, there was a lot of activity around Lorie Lounger's place.

She had been calling out for Bettina, and was concerned when she got no answer. Lorie felt it was time for her to leave, too, but had no idea where to start.

Once again, she called on her friends in the ant colony and they came running in force.

"I feel that it's time to get out of here, but there's no doorway," she declared impatiently.

"Right. You're supposed to make an opening when you're ready," one of the ants explained.

"Oh, but that sounds like work! Please do it for me? Pretty please?" Lorie begged.

Antoine gathered his group together for a meeting. "Sometimes we must say 'NO'—no matter how difficult it might be."

Antoine and most of the colony wished Lorie the best and left. Some found it too hard to ignore her pleadings and stayed.

"Well, we probably shouldn't," said one of the ants. "But we'll do it this one time."

The ants got busy. Lorie lounged in the dreamy darkness.

Over in the meadow, Bettina was thrilled with her new talent and fluttered from flower to flower.

In the quiet sun-drenched afternoon, she heard something coming from a ruby-red rose. As the butterfly looked up, she recognized the yellow and black furry body.

"Buzz," she called out, "take a break from pollinating and come say hi."

"Oh, it's you, Bettina! I saw some magnificent wings fly past me a while back and wondered who was so lucky!"

"Yes, it's me. Same me. New outfit. How have you been?"

"Just wonderful. Busy as usual, and I still adore my sweet-smelling job. Great seeing your smiling face."

The ants had worked hard and made good headway on Lorie Lounger's cocoon. Just as they were planning to quit for the day, her tiny house burst wide open.

Lorie blinked and looked around at the familiar forest. "This is fantastic! Now…uh, how do I get down from here?" she asked the group of ants.

"You can just spread your wings and fly like a… hey, wait a minute," one said. "I don't see any wings! In fact, your legs are barely there."

"Something is terribly wrong here," commented another ant.

"Is everything okay up here? My name is LB Junior. I was just wondering what…"

"There is a serious problem. Lorie Lounger is supposed to be able to fly, but she has no wings!"

"Did you build your strength up to break out, Lorie?"

"What do you mean? When I felt like exercising, I would rest 'til I got over it."

"Well, in order to develop your wings, it's vital that you work on breaking out while you're a chrysalis. It's a struggle, but that's how your wings grow and get strong enough to fly."

"But I didn't need to. I had all the help I needed from these industrious ants," Lorie insisted.

"Some things in life you must do on your own...like going through this struggle. Now, sadly, it's too late for you to have wings."

Lorie began to cry. "What can I do now? How will I even get down from this tree?"

"We thought we were helping, but we kept you grounded instead," one of the ants said for the group. "Let's get you down to safety, anyway."

The ants slowly carried her down to the ground, brought her a few drops of water on a petal and sorrowfully went on their way.

LB Junior stopped to check on Lorie as the sun was setting. "There's some hope," he said. "If you work on building up your tiny legs…you can at least get around that way. It's not flying, but it's better than nothing."

# Some things you must do on your own.

That night, she worked for the first time in her life…flexing and pushing her little legs into the base of the maple tree.

Near the fields, Bettina was excited to stop by for a visit with her old caterpillar friends.

"Well, look what the wind blew in," one of them said. "A most beautiful butterfly. "

"It's little ole me—Bettina."

"You're kidding!" they said in unison. "You just up and left us. We wondered where you went. How did you turn into a butterfly? And such a gorgeous one at that!"

"It's a new season. You're on the way!"

After sharing many laughs and stories, Bettina Butterfly curled up in a soft leaf nearby. She slept soundly all through the night.

At daybreak, Bettina flew over toward the old tree she had left. She saw a creature moving unsteadily around the base of it.

"You must love those extraordinary wings," came a distinctive voice.

"Lorie, is it you? I'm Bettina. It's nice to talk without a wall. How are you?"

"I'd be a lot better if I had worked like you did. I learned my lesson. That's why I'm exercising right now."

"Good for you. It's never too late to learn something new. Take care. See you later."

# It's never too late to learn something new.

Time passed and the maturing Ms. Butterfly had now become a flying whiz.

She winged her way to a field way deep in the forest. It was exquisite, but nothing looked familiar. An old, abandoned castle was a perfect backdrop for the most robust daisies and wild roses she had ever seen.

Bettina was so happy, she sang as she flew...remembering the sweet, old melody she had sung with the birds.

She slowly fluttered over to one flower, then another, until she noticed a butterfly trying to catch up with her.

"Bet...Bettina!!!" said a mature but exuberant voice.

Bettina looked back, mystified. "Buster! Buster! Could it be you?" she asked joyfully.

"I recognized your song. It's from your soul. Oh, I'm so happy to see you!"

He continued, "You were right all along. I do have choices. Thank you! Thank you! That rough pathway was no picnic, but it was truly a life-saver."

"Tell me ALL about it, Buster."

"Well, I really hit the very bottom—rock bottom. I was ready to give up completely, when I met a grasshopper. Guy Green said that the only way out was to take action."

"Yes, and…"

"I got so desperate, it was do or die. I did it! Right through the fear that held me back for so long.

"Boy, did I have some close calls…a treacherous wind storm, an unhappy snake, a biting bug. But, I survived, and met some good folks and had some amazing experiences along the way."

They talked and shared for many hours—and promised to always stay close.

Bettina felt so grateful as she flew back to her familiar meadow. She soon found the patch of Morning Glories where Ladybug was buried. She stopped at several blooms until she came to the most brilliant blue one.

There, cradled in the flower, was a gorgeous white feather.

Bettina laughed and cried at the same time. Yes, this was like a kiss from heaven.

And the mother butterfly left two eggs in the middle of a damp leaf. She lightly flew away toward the clear, blue sky.

It takes
strength
to survive.
It takes
courage
to live!

# The Music

Music is the color of life. The accompanying songs
complement the story...yet they stand on their own.
We hope the inspiring lyrics touch your heart.

# The Artists

### Lead Vocals:
Roy Clark
Bobby Bare
Tabitha Fair
Carol Grace Anderson

### Keyboards:
Lois Griscom Anderson
Jay Vernalli

### Guitar:
Danny Parks

### Violins:
Larry Franklin

### Bass:
Jon Vogt

### Drums:
Jerry Croon

### Background Vocals:
Lisa Silver
Vicki Hampton
Carol Grace Anderson

### Engineer:
Jay Vernalli

# We All Start Somewhere

*Artist: Roy Clark*
*Writers: Debbie Hupp*
*Carol Grace Anderson*

See the light
Through the stained glass window
How lovely the colors dance
It's hard to believe it
Someone could conceive it
From one little grain of sand

Watch that old river winding
Slowly rolling away
She how she's flowing
Forever growing
From one little drop of rain

We all start somewhere
And sometimes it's a mystery how
But change can happen anywhere
And there's no better time than now

Lilies, violets and roses
There's magic in what we see
They smile at the sun
Yet they had begun
As one little crusty seed

# Still A Butterfly

*Artist: Carol Grace Anderson*
*Writers: Debbie Hupp*
*Carol Grace Anderson*

Little things that made her who she was
The gold in her hair
That mischievous smile
Every move she made she seemed to dance
Just the vision of it lingers for a while

As time goes on
When you love someone
The changes you see
Happen so subtly
That no matter what you see
Before your eyes
In her heart, she's still a butterfly

Little things that make her who she is
Her silvery hair
Her tender embrace
She's been my rock
As time keeps rolling on
She still has all the love
She gave away

# Don't Bug Me
## (Buster's Song)

*Artist: Bobby Bare*
*Writers: Carol Grace Anderson*
*Debbie Hupp*

I don't look on the bright side
It only hurts my eyes
Happiness is just a crock
It's misery in disguise
You can take your motivation
And your inspiration too
Dump it in a dumpster
With your health food and tofu

Don't bug me
Don't hug me
I'm positively negative
And that's okay with me
Don't bug me

I don't buy that psychobabble
It's crazy talk to me
I'm happily unhappy
And that's how it's gonna be
Don't hold your breath believing
You can save me from myself
You'll be the first to know
If I turn into someone else

# We Can Fly
## (The Bumblebee Song)

*Artist: Tabitha Fair*
*Writers: Lisa Martin Palas*
*Carol Grace Anderson*

No one told the little bumblebee
She wouldn't be able to fly
So she just went
And spread her wings
Just like you and I

We can fly
Like the bumblebee
Yes, you and me
We can fly
Make our wildest dreams reality
We can fly

There's no limit
To what we can do
When we believe that we can
There are so many possibilities
Once we understand

## All Through The Night
## Welsh lullaby

*Artist: Lois Griscom Anderson*

This peaceful melody sounds like it was meant to be Bettina's song. It's a lovely old lullaby arranged by the pianist...Lois Anderson.

She's an accomplished musician, teacher, and music director of Mountainville Methodist Church in New York.

Lois was the soloist and musical arranger for inspirational radio and television programs starting in the 1950's. The programs were hosted by her husband Jim. They're my marvelous Mom and Dad.

Also available from Rock Hill Publishing
are Carol Grace Anderson's:


**Get Fired Up Without Burning Out!**
*A 178-page book that will motivate and
inspire you to get and stay fired up!*
$14.95


**Get Fired Up!... Songs**
*This is a 10-song CD with upbeat music
to motivate...and keep you going!*
$10


**Some Angels Have Four Paws
(Life Lessons From Our Dogs)**
*A beautiful hardcover gift book that
will touch your heart and spirit.*
$14.95


**Butterfly Factor Music**
*The CD collection of original songs
that accompany this book.*
$10


Order toll-free by phone:
**877-446-9364**


Or visit our secure website and order online:
**Butterflyfactor.com**

## About the author:

Carol Grace Anderson is a former Psychology teacher. She's now a highly successful song-writer, producer, entertainer, and is a consultant for the legendary artist, Roy Clark.

Carol's a member of the Screen Actors Guild, ASCAP, and the National Speakers Association.

Her books have encouraged and empowered lives all over the country and internationally. They've recently been translated into Greek, Chinese and Croatian.

She's a national motivational speaker and her message has empowered thousands.